EMMANUEL JOSEPH

Sustainable Enterprise Development:
Business Analysis and Management

Copyright © 2025 by Emmanuel Joseph

All rights reserved. No part of this publication may be reproduced, stored or transmitted in any form or by any means, electronic, mechanical, photocopying, recording, scanning, or otherwise without written permission from the publisher. It is illegal to copy this book, post it to a website, or distribute it by any other means without permission.

First edition

*This book was professionally typeset on Reedsy.
Find out more at reedsy.com*

Contents

1   Chapter 1   1
2   Chapter 1: Understanding Business Analysis   3
3   Chapter 2: The Role of a Business Analyst   5
4   Chapter 3: Stakeholder Engagement and Management   7
5   Chapter 4: Gathering and Documenting Requirements   9
6   Chapter 5: Process Mapping and Analysis   11
7   Chapter 6: Data Analysis and Decision Making   13
8   Chapter 7: Solution Design and Implementation   15
9   Chapter 8: Change Management and Communication   17
10   Chapter 9: Performance Measurement and Evaluation   19
11   Chapter 10: Risk Management and Mitigation   21
12   Chapter 11: Leveraging Technology in Business Analysis   23
13   Chapter 12: Continuous Improvement and Future Trends   25

1

Chapter 1

Introduction

In the fast-paced world of modern business, the ability to analyze and manage business processes effectively is paramount to success. "Scaling Heights: A Comprehensive Guide to Business Analysis and Management" seeks to equip readers with the knowledge and skills required to excel in this crucial domain. This guide will cover everything from fundamental concepts to advanced techniques, ensuring a well-rounded understanding of business analysis and management. Throughout the book, we will explore real-world examples and case studies to illustrate the principles and practices discussed.

This book is designed for a diverse audience, including aspiring business analysts, seasoned professionals looking to refine their skills, and business managers aiming to improve their strategic decision-making. Each chapter will delve into a specific aspect of business analysis and management, providing readers with a comprehensive toolkit for tackling various business challenges. By the end of this journey, readers will have a solid foundation in business analysis and management, enabling them to drive positive change within their organizations.

As we embark on this journey, it is essential to recognize the interconnectedness of business analysis and management. These disciplines are not isolated silos but rather interdependent functions that work together to achieve organizational goals. Effective business analysis informs sound management decisions, while robust management practices create an environment conducive to successful analysis. This holistic approach will be a recurring theme throughout the book, emphasizing the importance of integration and collaboration.

So, whether you are just starting your career or looking to enhance your existing skills, "Scaling Heights" will provide you with valuable insights and practical guidance. Let's embark on this journey together and unlock the potential of business analysis and management to transform your organization.

2

Chapter 1: Understanding Business Analysis

Business analysis is the practice of identifying business needs and determining solutions to business problems. It involves a detailed examination of business processes, systems, and organizational structures to understand how they can be improved. This chapter introduces the core principles of business analysis, including the role of a business analyst, the importance of stakeholder engagement, and various techniques used to gather and analyze information.

The first step in business analysis is to understand the business context and objectives. This involves identifying the key stakeholders and their needs, as well as understanding the current business processes and systems. A business analyst must communicate effectively with stakeholders to gather accurate information and build a clear picture of the business environment.

Once the business context is understood, the next step is to identify areas for improvement. This can involve analyzing current processes to pinpoint inefficiencies, gathering data to support decision-making, and developing solutions to address business problems. Effective business analysis requires a combination of analytical skills, communication skills, and problem-solving abilities.

Throughout this chapter, we will explore various techniques and tools used in business analysis, such as SWOT analysis, process mapping, and requirements gathering. By the end of this chapter, readers will have a solid foundation in the fundamentals of business analysis, setting the stage for more advanced topics in subsequent chapters.

3

Chapter 2: The Role of a Business Analyst

The role of a business analyst is multifaceted, involving various responsibilities that contribute to the successful implementation of business solutions. In this chapter, we will explore the key functions and skills required for a business analyst, highlighting the importance of communication, critical thinking, and adaptability. Business analysts act as the bridge between stakeholders and technical teams, ensuring that business needs are accurately captured and translated into actionable requirements.

One of the primary responsibilities of a business analyst is to facilitate effective communication among stakeholders. This involves conducting interviews, workshops, and meetings to gather information and understand stakeholder needs. A business analyst must be able to listen actively, ask probing questions, and synthesize information from diverse sources. Effective communication is essential for building trust and ensuring that all parties have a shared understanding of project goals and objectives.

Critical thinking and problem-solving skills are also crucial for a business analyst. They must be able to analyze complex business processes, identify inefficiencies, and propose viable solutions. This requires a deep understanding of the business environment, as well as the ability to think strategically and consider the long-term implications of proposed changes. Business analysts must also be adept at using various analytical tools and techniques to support their decision-making.

Adaptability is another key attribute of a successful business analyst. In a rapidly changing business landscape, analysts must be able to respond to evolving requirements and shifting priorities. This may involve revisiting initial assumptions, refining requirements, and working closely with stakeholders to ensure that solutions remain aligned with business objectives. By staying flexible and open to new ideas, business analysts can help organizations navigate change and achieve their goals.

4

Chapter 3: Stakeholder Engagement and Management

Engaging and managing stakeholders is a critical aspect of business analysis. In this chapter, we will discuss the importance of stakeholder engagement, the different types of stakeholders, and strategies for effective stakeholder management. By building strong relationships with stakeholders, business analysts can ensure that projects are aligned with business needs and that any potential issues are addressed promptly.

Stakeholders can be categorized into several groups, including internal stakeholders (such as employees and managers) and external stakeholders (such as customers, suppliers, and regulators). Each group has unique interests and perspectives, which must be taken into account during the business analysis process. A thorough understanding of stakeholder needs and expectations is essential for ensuring that solutions are well-received and effective.

Effective stakeholder engagement involves proactive communication and collaboration. Business analysts must be skilled at facilitating discussions, managing conflicts, and building consensus. This can involve using various techniques, such as stakeholder interviews, surveys, focus groups, and workshops. By actively involving stakeholders in the analysis process, business analysts can gather valuable insights and foster a sense of ownership and commitment to the project's success.

Managing stakeholder expectations is also a crucial aspect of stakeholder engagement. Business analysts must set clear expectations regarding project goals, timelines, and deliverables. This involves providing regular updates, addressing concerns promptly, and ensuring that stakeholders are kept informed throughout the project lifecycle. By managing expectations effectively, business analysts can build trust and maintain strong relationships with stakeholders.

5

Chapter 4: Gathering and Documenting Requirements

A crucial part of business analysis is gathering and documenting requirements. This chapter delves into the techniques and best practices for eliciting requirements from stakeholders and documenting them in a clear and concise manner. Proper requirements gathering ensures that the final solution meets the business needs and avoids costly rework down the line.

The process of gathering requirements begins with identifying the key stakeholders and understanding their needs and expectations. Various techniques can be used to elicit requirements, including interviews, surveys, focus groups, and observation. Each technique has its strengths and weaknesses, and the choice of method depends on the specific context and objectives of the project.

Once the requirements have been gathered, the next step is to document them in a way that is easily understandable and accessible to all stakeholders. This involves creating requirements documents, such as business requirements documents (BRDs), functional requirements documents (FRDs), and use cases. Clear and concise documentation is essential for ensuring that all stakeholders have a shared understanding of the project scope and objectives.

Effective requirements management also involves validating and prioritizing requirements. This involves reviewing the requirements with stakeholders to ensure they accurately reflect their needs and expectations. Prioritization helps to identify the most critical requirements and allocate resources accordingly. By following best practices in requirements gathering and documentation, business analysts can ensure the successful delivery of projects.

6

Chapter 5: Process Mapping and Analysis

Process mapping and analysis are essential tools for understanding and improving business processes. In this chapter, we will explore the techniques and tools used to create process maps, analyze process flows, and identify opportunities for improvement. Process mapping provides a visual representation of business processes, making it easier to identify inefficiencies and areas for optimization.

The first step in process mapping is to define the scope of the process to be analyzed. This involves identifying the key inputs, outputs, and stakeholders involved in the process. Process maps can be created using various techniques, such as flowcharts, swimlane diagrams, and value stream mapping. Each technique has its strengths and is suited to different types of processes.

Once the process map is created, the next step is to analyze the process to identify areas for improvement. This involves examining each step in the process to identify bottlenecks, redundancies, and inefficiencies. Techniques such as root cause analysis, gap analysis, and benchmarking can be used to support this analysis.

Improvement opportunities identified through process mapping and analysis can lead to significant gains in efficiency, quality, and customer satisfaction. By understanding and optimizing business processes, organizations can achieve better outcomes and drive continuous improvement. This chapter provides readers with the tools and techniques needed to conduct effective process mapping and analysis.

7

Chapter 6: Data Analysis and Decision Making

D ata analysis is a critical component of business analysis, providing the foundation for informed decision-making. In this chapter, we will discuss the importance of data analysis, the different types of data, and the techniques used to analyze data. By leveraging data effectively, business analysts can support strategic decision-making and drive business success.

The first step in data analysis is to collect and organize data from various sources. This can include structured data, such as sales figures and financial reports, as well as unstructured data, such as customer feedback and social media posts. Business analysts must be skilled at using tools and techniques to gather and process data, ensuring that it is accurate and relevant.

Once the data is collected, the next step is to analyze it to identify trends, patterns, and insights. Various techniques can be used for data analysis, including descriptive statistics, inferential statistics, and data visualization. Business analysts must be able to interpret the results of their analysis and communicate their findings effectively to stakeholders.

Effective data analysis supports decision-making by providing evidence-based insights that can be used to inform strategy and drive business success. This chapter provides readers with the knowledge and skills needed to conduct data analysis and make informed decisions. By leveraging data effectively, business analysts can help organizations achieve their goals and stay competitive in a rapidly changing business environment.

8

Chapter 7: Solution Design and Implementation

Designing and implementing solutions is a critical aspect of business analysis. In this chapter, we will explore the process of developing and deploying effective solutions to address business needs. This involves collaborating with stakeholders to define solution requirements, creating detailed design specifications, and overseeing the implementation process to ensure that the solution meets business objectives.

The solution design process begins with defining the requirements and creating a high-level design. This involves working closely with stakeholders to ensure that the solution aligns with their needs and expectations. Detailed design specifications are then created, outlining the technical and functional aspects of the solution. Business analysts must be skilled at translating business requirements into actionable design documents.

Once the design is complete, the next step is to implement the solution. This involves coordinating with various teams, such as development, testing, and operations, to ensure that the solution is built and deployed effectively. Business analysts play a crucial role in overseeing the implementation process, providing guidance and support to ensure that the solution meets quality standards and delivers the desired outcomes.

Throughout the implementation process, it is essential to monitor progress and address any issues that arise. This involves conducting regular reviews, managing risks, and ensuring that stakeholders are kept informed of project status. By following best practices in solution design and implementation, business analysts can help organizations achieve successful outcomes and drive continuous improvement.

9

Chapter 8: Change Management and Communication

Effective change management is essential for ensuring that business solutions are successfully adopted and integrated into the organization. In this chapter, we will discuss the principles of change management, the importance of effective communication, and strategies for managing resistance to change. By fostering a culture of change readiness, business analysts can support the successful implementation of business solutions.

Change management involves preparing, supporting, and guiding individuals and teams through the process of change. This begins with creating a clear vision for the change and communicating its benefits to stakeholders. Business analysts must be skilled at crafting compelling messages and delivering them through various channels to ensure that all stakeholders are informed and engaged.

Managing resistance to change is a critical aspect of change management. People are often resistant to change due to fear of the unknown, concerns about their ability to adapt, or a lack of understanding of the change's benefits. Business analysts can address these concerns by providing training, resources, and support to help stakeholders navigate the change process. This involves creating a supportive environment that encourages open communication and feedback.

Effective communication is the cornerstone of successful change management. This involves delivering clear, consistent messages and actively listening to stakeholder feedback. Business analysts must be skilled at using various communication techniques, such as presentations, workshops, and one-on-one meetings, to ensure that stakeholders are informed and engaged. By fostering a culture of open communication and collaboration, business analysts can support the successful adoption of business solutions.

10

Chapter 9: Performance Measurement and Evaluation

Measuring and evaluating performance is essential for assessing the success of business solutions and identifying areas for improvement. In this chapter, we will explore the importance of performance measurement, the different types of performance metrics, and techniques for evaluating performance. By establishing a robust performance measurement framework, business analysts can support continuous improvement and drive business success.

Performance measurement involves defining key performance indicators (KPIs) and tracking progress against these metrics. This begins with identifying the critical success factors for the business solution and selecting appropriate KPIs to measure performance. Business analysts must be skilled at using various tools and techniques to collect and analyze performance data.

Once the performance data is collected, the next step is to evaluate the results and identify areas for improvement. This involves comparing actual performance against target metrics, conducting root cause analysis to identify the underlying causes of performance gaps, and developing action plans to address these gaps. Business analysts must be able to interpret performance data and provide actionable insights to stakeholders.

Effective performance evaluation also involves conducting regular reviews and providing feedback to stakeholders. This ensures that performance issues are promptly addressed, and continuous improvement efforts are supported. By establishing a robust performance measurement framework, business analysts can help organizations achieve their goals and drive business success.

Chapter 10: Risk Management and Mitigation

Managing risks is a critical aspect of business analysis, ensuring that potential issues are identified and addressed before they become significant problems. In this chapter, we will discuss the principles of risk management, the different types of risks, and strategies for mitigating risks. By proactively managing risks, business analysts can support the successful implementation of business solutions.

Risk management involves identifying, assessing, and prioritizing risks, and developing strategies to mitigate them. This begins with conducting a thorough risk assessment to identify potential risks and evaluate their likelihood and impact. Business analysts must be skilled at using various risk assessment techniques, such as SWOT analysis, risk matrices, and scenario planning.

Once the risks are identified, the next step is to develop risk mitigation strategies. This involves creating action plans to address the most critical risks, such as implementing preventive measures, developing contingency plans, and allocating resources to manage risks. Business analysts must be able to communicate risk mitigation plans effectively to stakeholders and ensure that they are implemented.

Effective risk management also involves monitoring and reviewing risks throughout the project lifecycle. This ensures that new risks are identified and addressed promptly, and that existing risks are managed effectively. By following best practices in risk management, business analysts can help organizations navigate uncertainty and achieve successful outcomes.

12

Chapter 11: Leveraging Technology in Business Analysis

In the digital age, leveraging technology is crucial for enhancing business analysis and management practices. In this chapter, we will explore various technological tools and platforms that can support business analysis activities, such as data analytics software, project management tools, and collaborative platforms. By integrating technology into their workflows, business analysts can improve efficiency, accuracy, and collaboration.

One of the most impactful technologies in business analysis is data analytics software. Tools like Microsoft Power BI, Tableau, and Google Analytics allow business analysts to collect, process, and visualize data, providing valuable insights that inform decision-making. These tools enable analysts to identify trends, patterns, and anomalies in data, helping organizations make data-driven decisions.

Project management tools, such as Microsoft Project, Trello, and Asana, are also essential for business analysts. These platforms provide a structured approach to managing projects, from planning and scheduling to tracking progress and reporting. By using project management tools, business analysts can ensure that projects are delivered on time, within scope, and within budget.

Collaborative platforms, such as Microsoft Teams, Slack, and SharePoint, facilitate communication and collaboration among stakeholders. These tools enable real-time communication, document sharing, and collaboration, ensuring that all team members are aligned and informed. By leveraging technology, business analysts can enhance their productivity and drive better outcomes for their organizations.

13

Chapter 12: Continuous Improvement and Future Trends

Continuous improvement is a fundamental principle of business analysis and management. In this final chapter, we will discuss the importance of fostering a culture of continuous improvement, the methods for driving ongoing improvements, and the future trends that will shape the field of business analysis. By embracing continuous improvement, organizations can stay competitive and adapt to changing market conditions.

Continuous improvement involves regularly evaluating and refining business processes, systems, and strategies to achieve better outcomes. This can be achieved through various methodologies, such as Lean, Six Sigma, and Agile. Business analysts play a crucial role in driving continuous improvement efforts by identifying opportunities for optimization and implementing changes that deliver measurable benefits.

Fostering a culture of continuous improvement requires a commitment to learning and innovation. Organizations must encourage employees to seek out new ideas, experiment with innovative approaches, and share their insights with others. Business analysts can support this culture by promoting best practices, providing training and development opportunities, and facilitating knowledge sharing across teams.

Looking ahead, several trends are poised to shape the future of business analysis. The increasing adoption of artificial intelligence (AI) and machine learning (ML) will enable more advanced data analysis and decision-making capabilities. The rise of digital transformation initiatives will drive the need for business analysts to navigate complex technological landscapes. Additionally, the growing emphasis on sustainability and social responsibility will require business analysts to consider the broader impact of their recommendations.

By staying abreast of these trends and continuously improving their skills, business analysts can remain valuable contributors to their organizations' success. As we conclude "Scaling Heights: A Comprehensive Guide to Business Analysis and Management," we hope that readers are equipped with the knowledge and tools needed to excel in this dynamic field and drive meaningful change within their organizations.

Conclusion

"Scaling Heights" concludes by reinforcing the importance of continuous improvement and staying ahead of future trends in business analysis and management. Embracing a culture of continuous improvement allows organizations to adapt to changing market conditions and maintain a competitive edge. Business analysts play a vital role in driving these efforts by identifying opportunities for optimization and implementing innovative solutions. As we look to the future, trends such as artificial intelligence, digital transformation, and sustainability will shape the field, requiring business analysts to stay abreast of new developments and continuously enhance their skills.

By integrating the knowledge and tools provided in this guide, readers will be well-equipped to tackle various business challenges and drive meaningful change within their organizations. "Scaling Heights" offers a comprehensive roadmap for mastering business analysis and management, empowering readers to achieve their professional goals and contribute to their organization's success.

www.ingramcontent.com/pod-product-compliance
Lightning Source LLC
LaVergne TN
LVHW020742090526
838202LV00057BA/6188